Library of Congress Control Number: 2016907760
ISBN: 978-0-9908757-8-9

Published by Balafun
Bothell, WA
www.balafun.com

balafun

Gladys T. Kenfack

Illustrator: Daniel Minlo

Africa ABC

Hop on board; we are going to Africa!

Let's learn your ABCs on a fun ride.
Please keep your eyes opened wide.

There are great rivers that flow through the mountains.
We can see the animals at their best, running free.

Mount Kilimanjaro is the great mountain east,
and the great Sahara Desert is all the way north.

Now we go west to the mighty jungle,
If you are not careful, you may definitely stumble.

Then we head down south, too, if you don't mind.
There gold and diamonds we will find.

The lakes over there have some fun names,
Just like Lake Tanganyika.

The music of Africa is the call of the wild.
The true sound of nature, and it feels hot or mild.

There are so many new things to see,
From wild animals to the biggest tree.

What are you waiting for? Now turn the page.

A a

AaBbCc

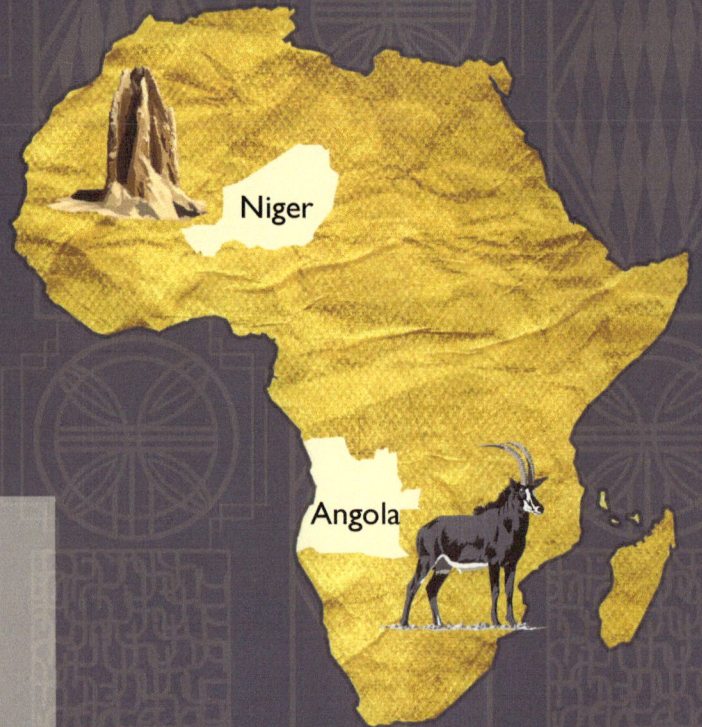

Niger

Angola

anthill

Antelope

B b

AaBbCc

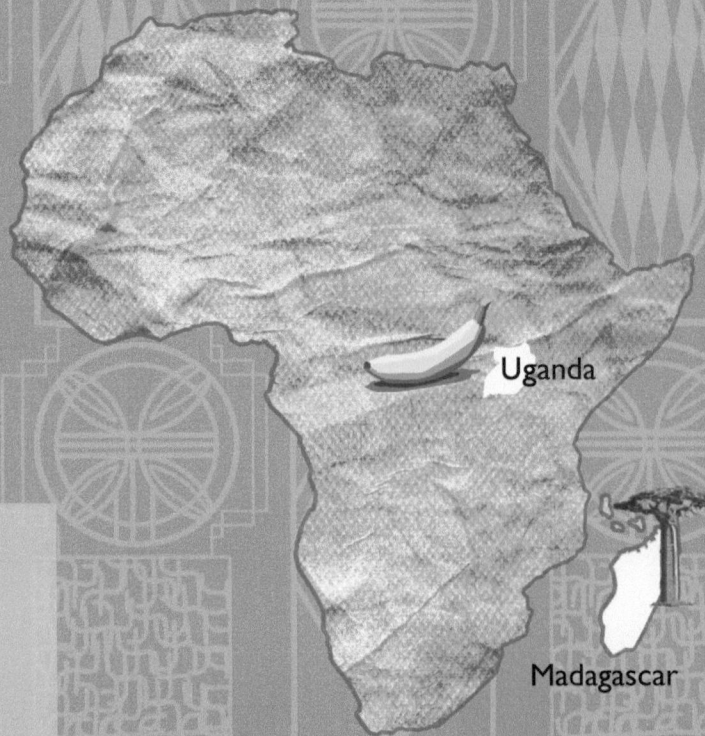

Uganda

Madagascar

banana

Baobab

C c

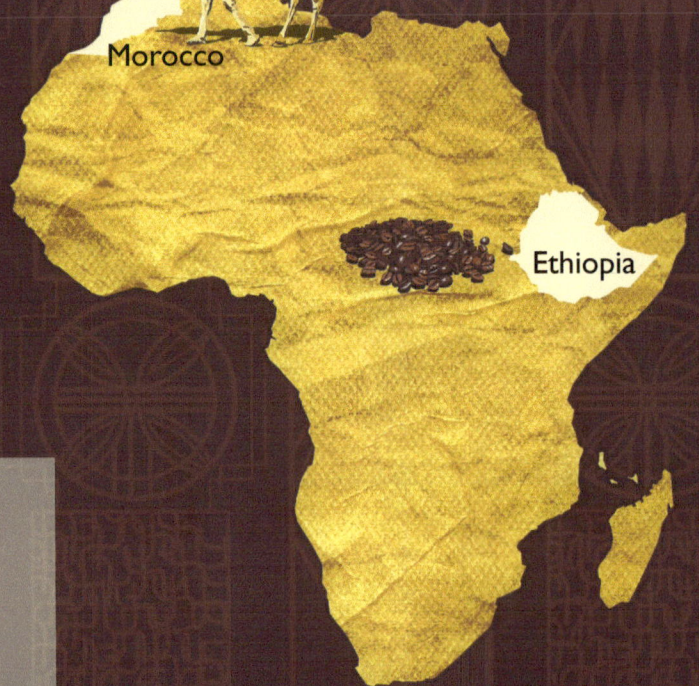

Morocco

Ethiopia

BbCcDd

camel

Coffee

D d

Tunisia

Morocco

Western Sahara

Algeria

Libya

Egypt

Mauritania

Mali

Niger

Chad

Sudan

Senegal

CcDdEe

desert

Djembe

E e

Togo

Zambia

DdEeFf

eagle

Elephant

F f

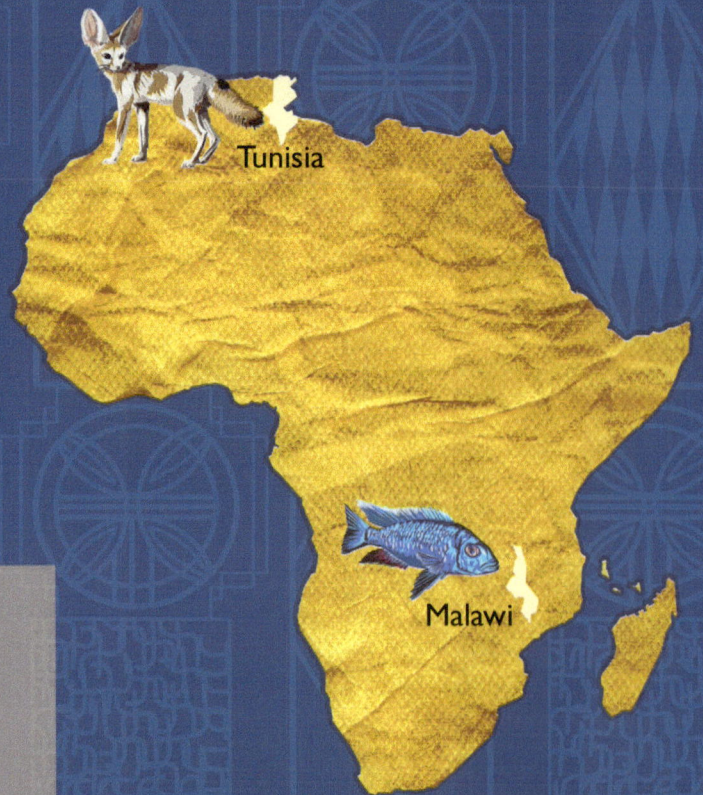

Tunisia

Malawi

EeFfGg

fennec

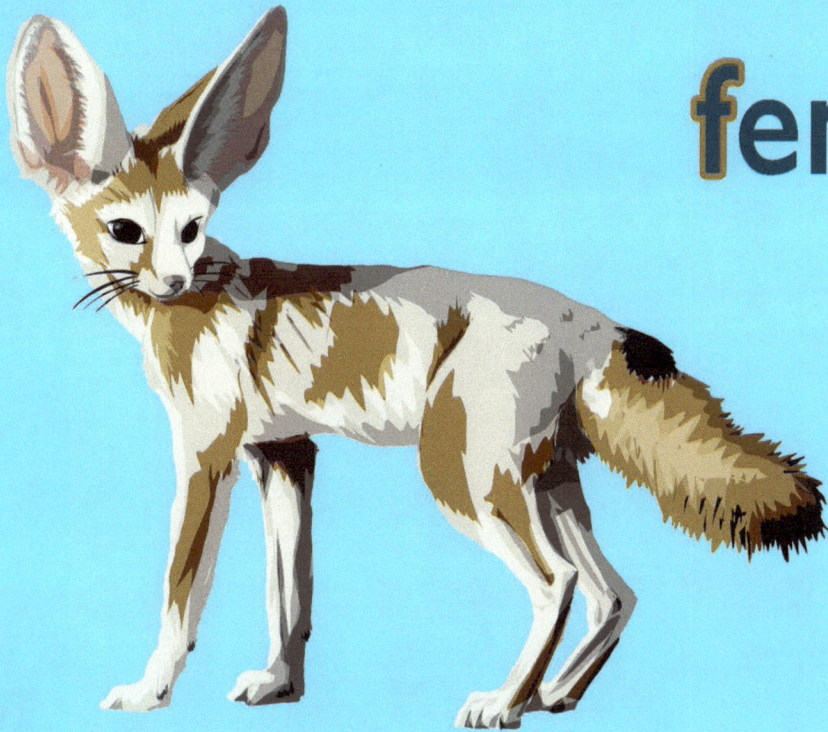

Fish

G g

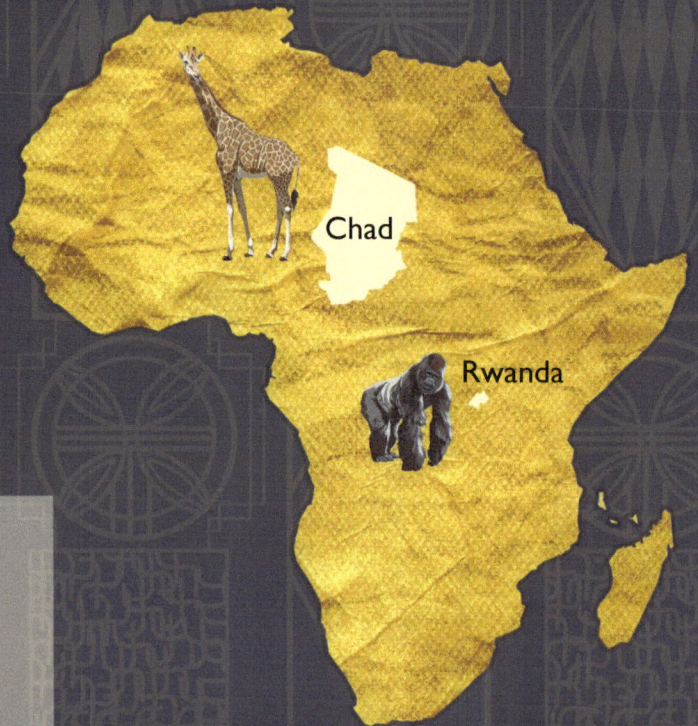

Chad

Rwanda

FfGgHh

Gorilla

giraffe

H h

Ginea

Cameroon

GgHhIi

hat

Hut

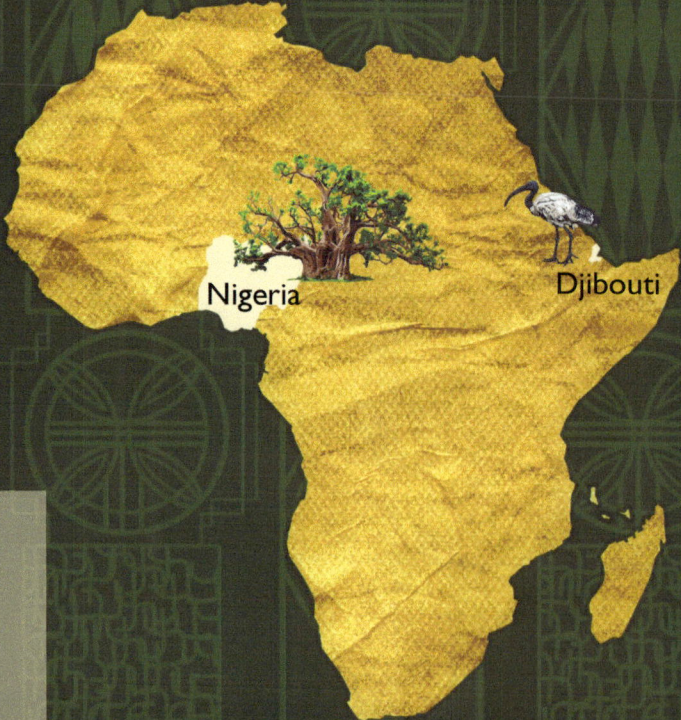

I i

Nigeria

Djibouti

HhIiJj

ibis

Iroko

J j

Central African Republic

Gabon

li Jj Kk

jackfruit

Jungle

K k

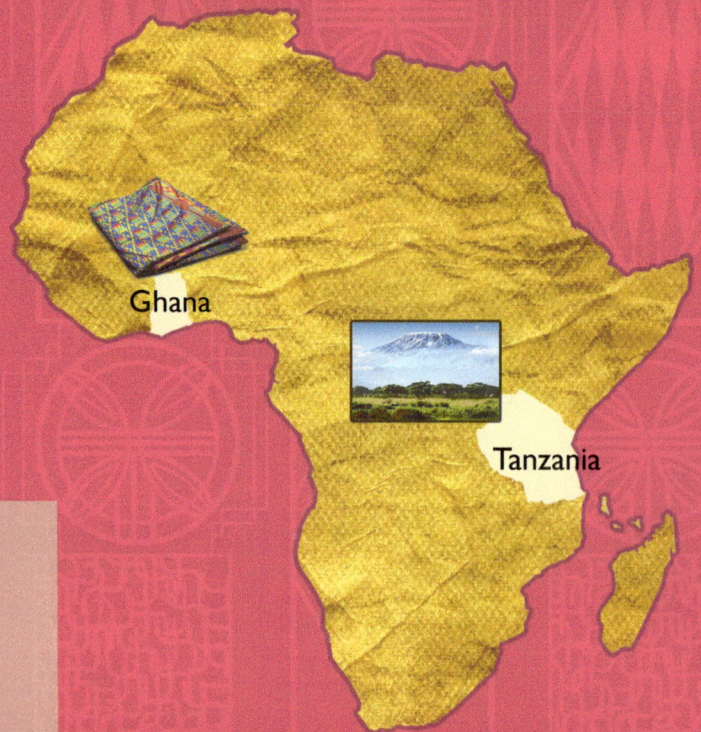

Ghana

Tanzania

JjKkLl

Kilimanjaro

kente

L l

Libya

Zimbabwe

KkLlMm

lake

Lion

M m

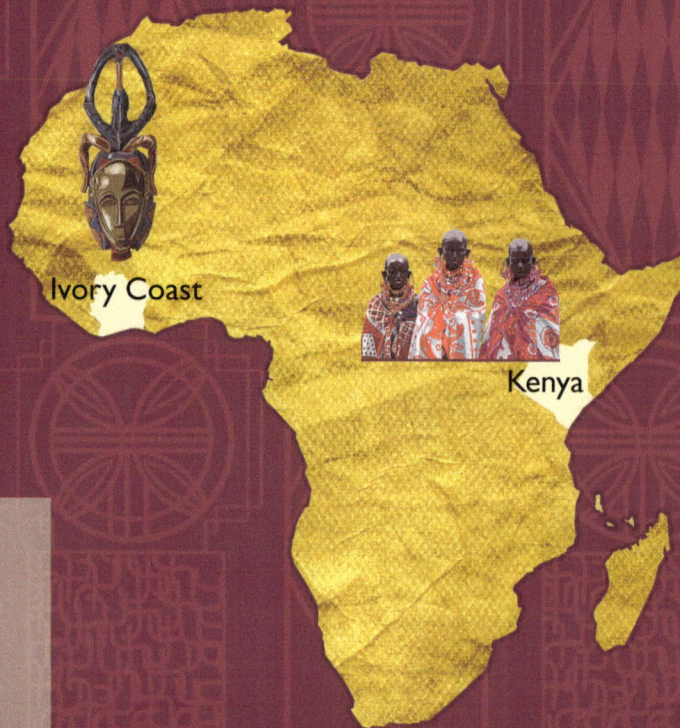

Ivory Coast

Kenya

Ll **Mm** Nn

mask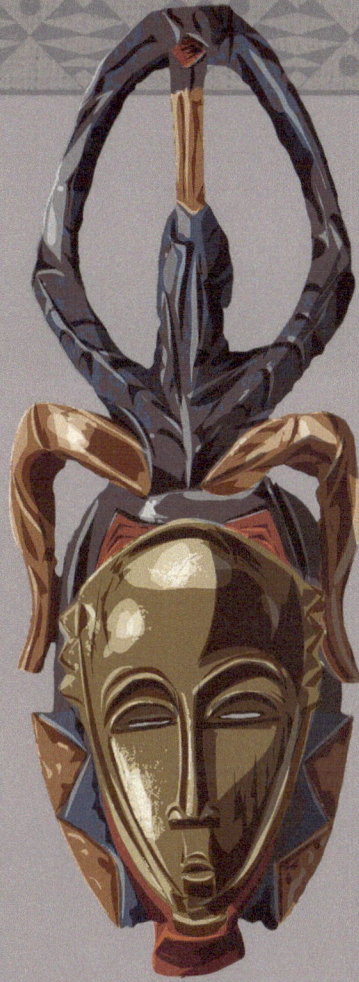

Maasai

N n

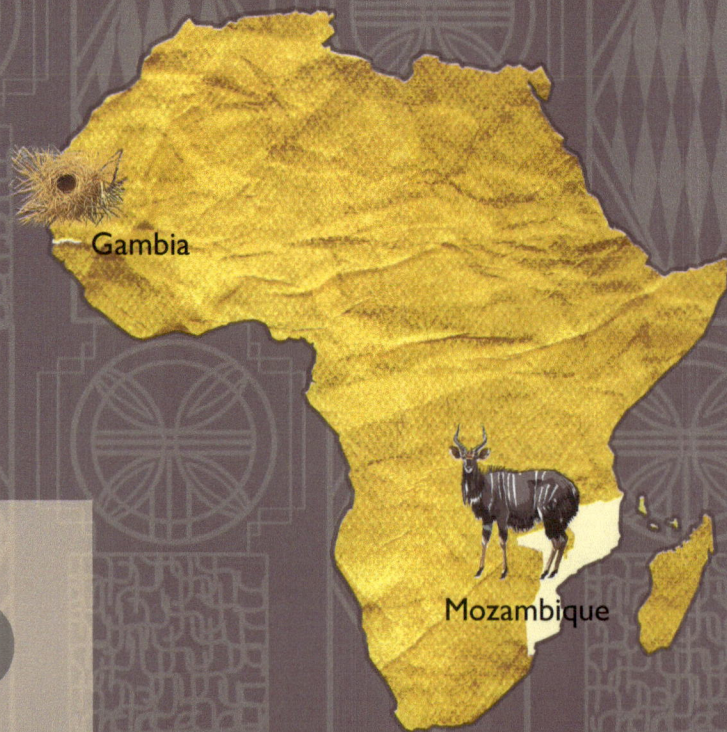

Gambia

Mozambique

MmNnOo

nest

Nyala

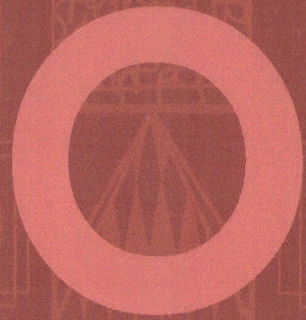

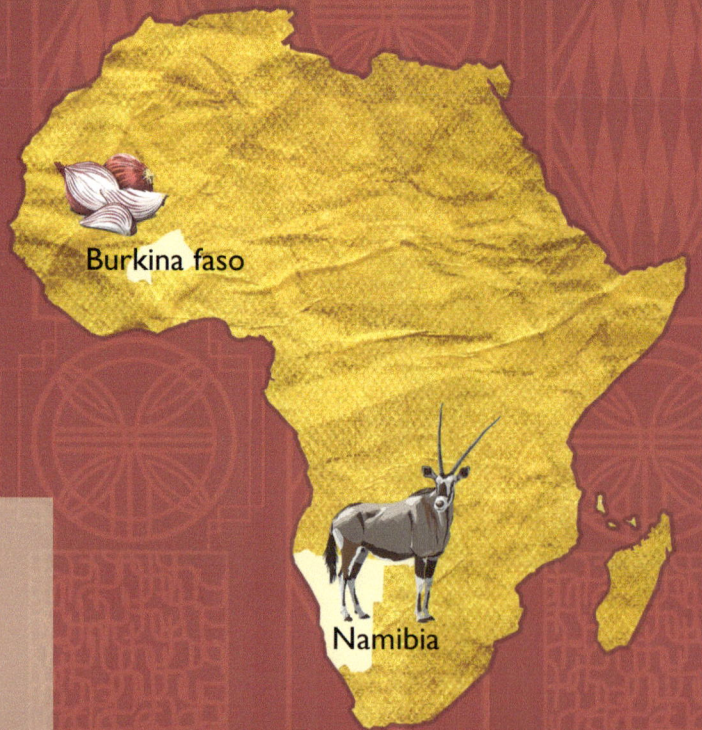

Oo

Burkina faso

Namibia

NnOoPp

Oryx

onion

P p

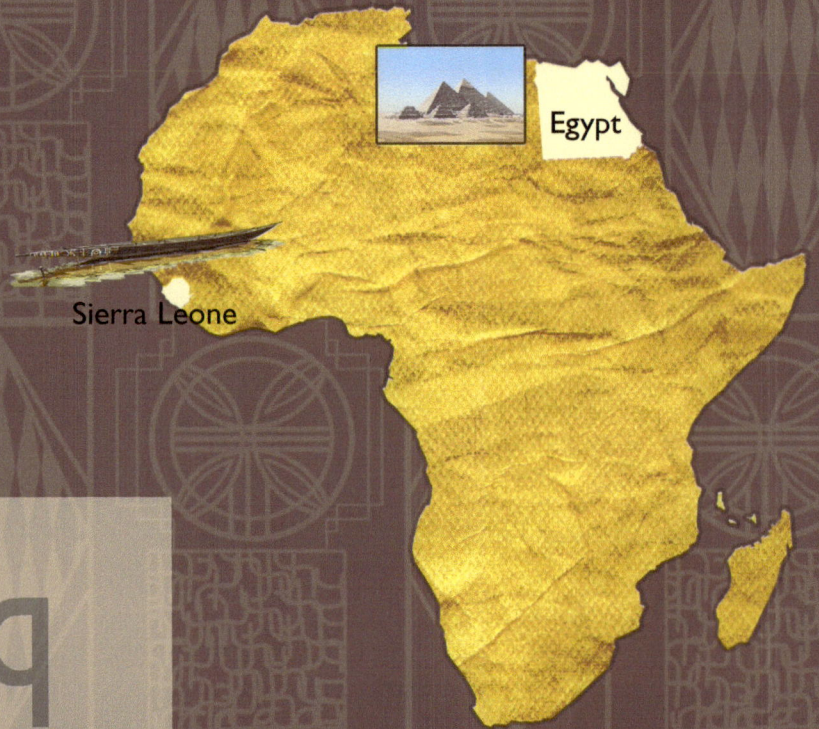

Egypt

Sierra Leone

OoPpQq

Pyramids

pirogue

Q q

Burundi

Comoros

PpQqRr

quail

Quagga

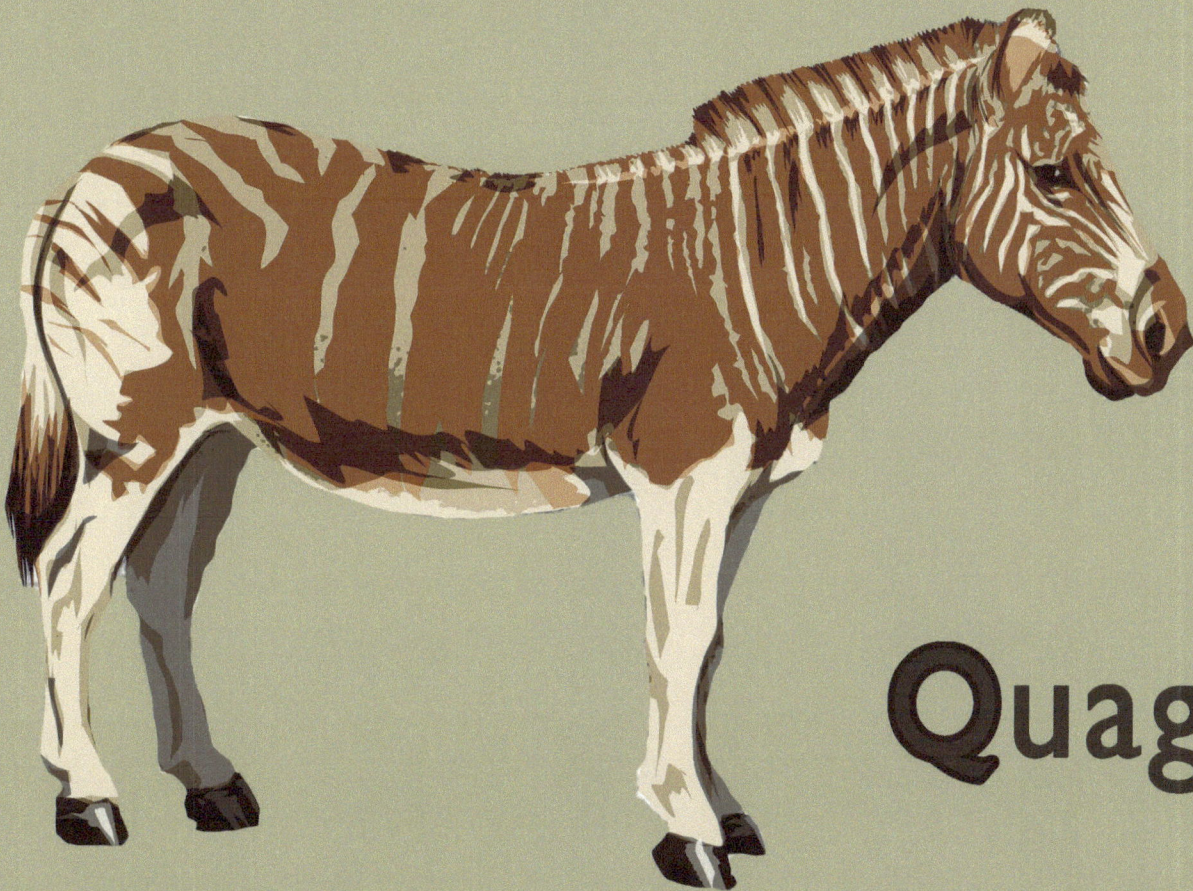

R r

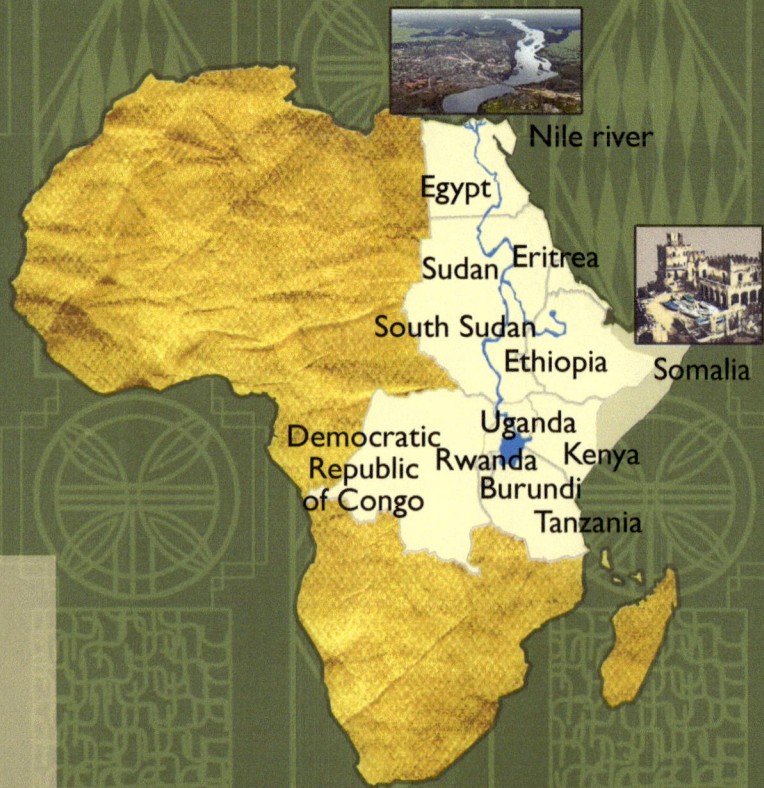

Nile river

Egypt

Sudan

Eritrea

South Sudan

Ethiopia

Somalia

Uganda

Democratic
Republic
of Congo

Rwanda

Kenya

Burundi

Tanzania

QqRrSs

ruins

River

S s

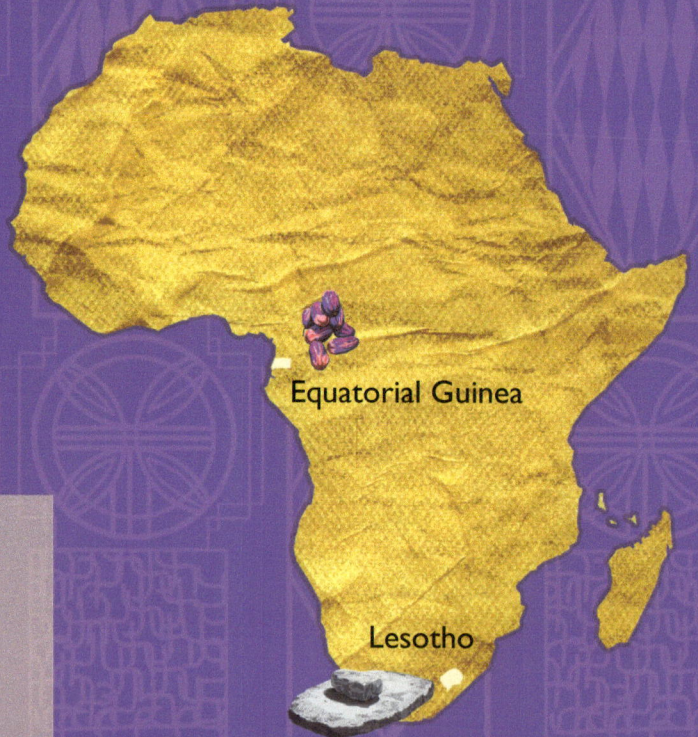

Equatorial Guinea

Lesotho

RrSsTt

Stone

safou

T t

SsTtUu

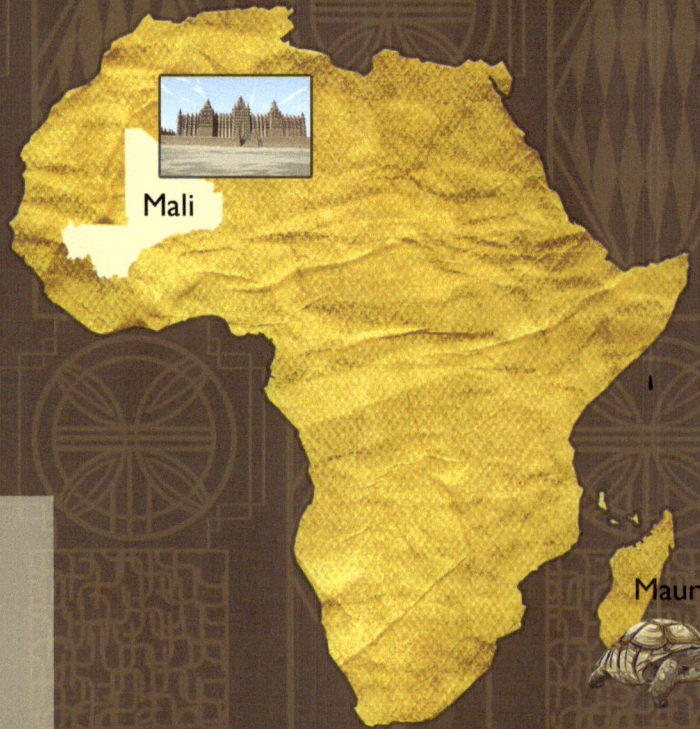

Mali

Mauritius

Timbuktu

tortoise

U u

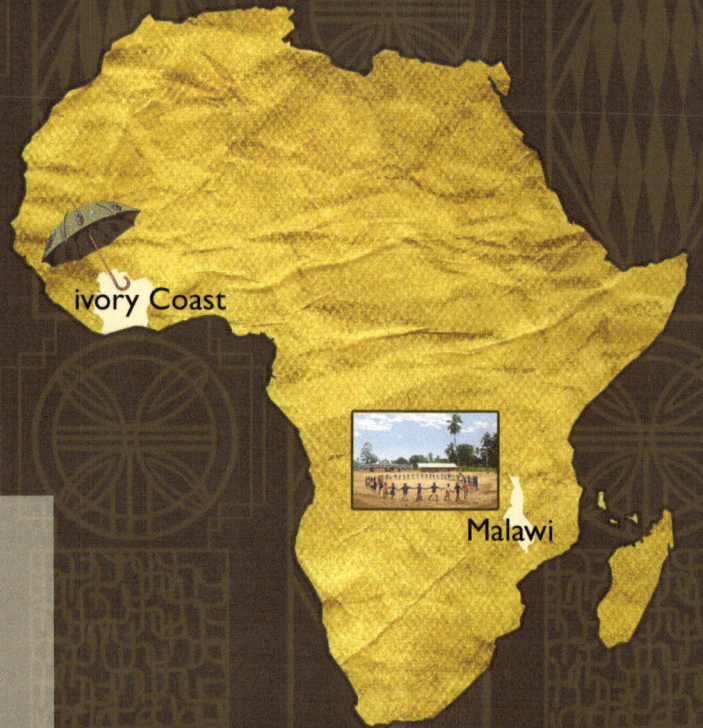

ivory Coast

Malawi

T t **U u** V v

umbrella

Ubuntu

Vv

Central African Republic

South Africa

Uu**Vv**Ww

Village

vuvuzela

W w

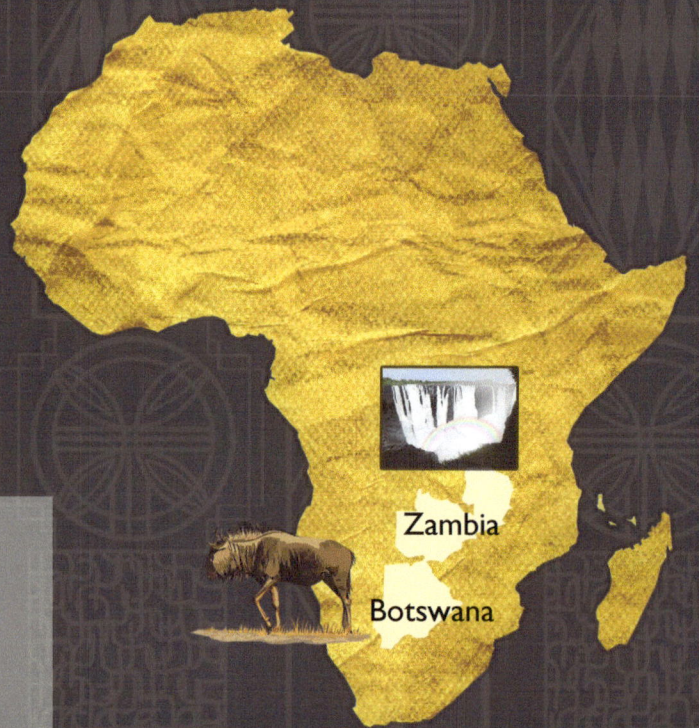

Zambia

Botswana

VvWwXx

wildebeest

Waterfall

X x

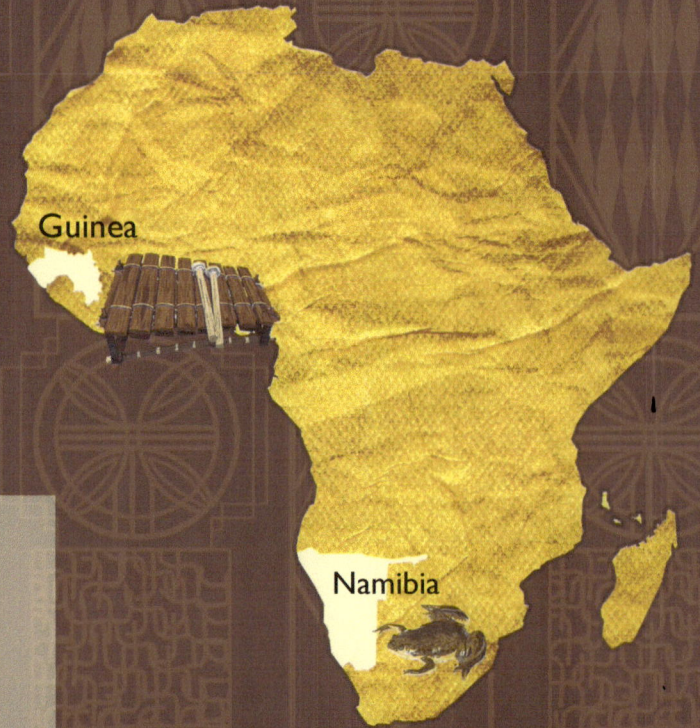

Guinea

Namibia

WwXxYy

Xylophone

xenopus

Y y

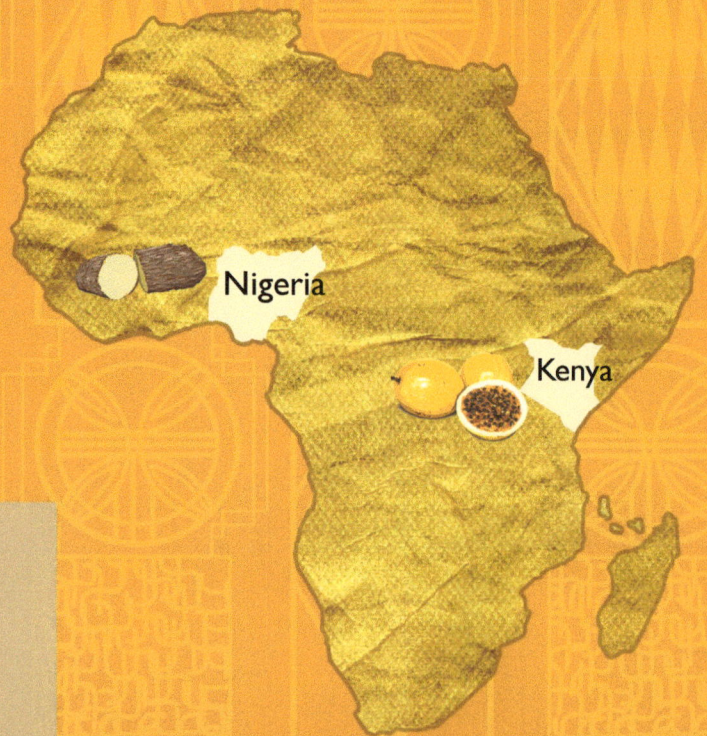

Nigeria

Kenya

XxYyZz

yams

Yellow Passion Fruit

Zz

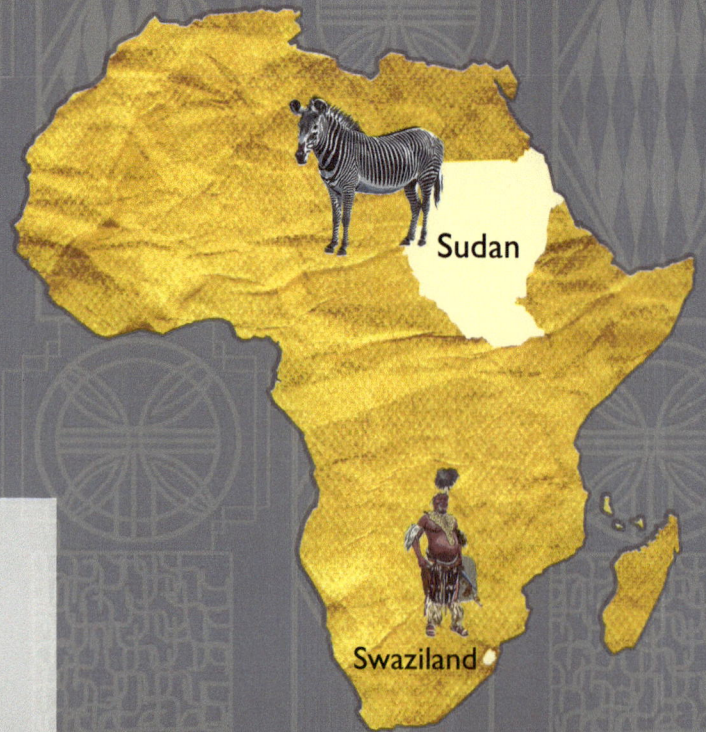

Sudan

Swaziland

YyZz

zebra

Zulu

Aa	Bb	Cc	Dd
Ee	Ff	Gg	Hh
Ii	Jj	Kk	Ll
Mm	Nn	Oo	Pp
Qq	Rr	Ss	Tt
Uu	Vv	Ww	Xx
Yy	Zz		

Tunizia

Nile River

Morocco

Algeria

Lybia

Egypt

Western Sahara

Mauritania

Mali

Niger

Chad

Sudan

Eritrea

Senegal
Gambia
Guinea Bissau
Guinea

Burkina Faso

Benin

Nigeria

Togo

Djibouti

Somalia

Sierra Leone

Lory Coast

Ethiopia

Liberia

Ghana

Cameroon

Central African
Republic

Equatorial Guinea

Congo

Uganda

Gabon

Kenya

Democratic
Republic
of Congo

Rwanda
Burundi

Cabinda
(Angola)

Tanzania

Comoros

Angola

Malawi

Zambia

Madagaskar

Namibia

Zimbabwe

Botwana

Mozambique

Mauritius

Swaziland

Lesotho

South Africa

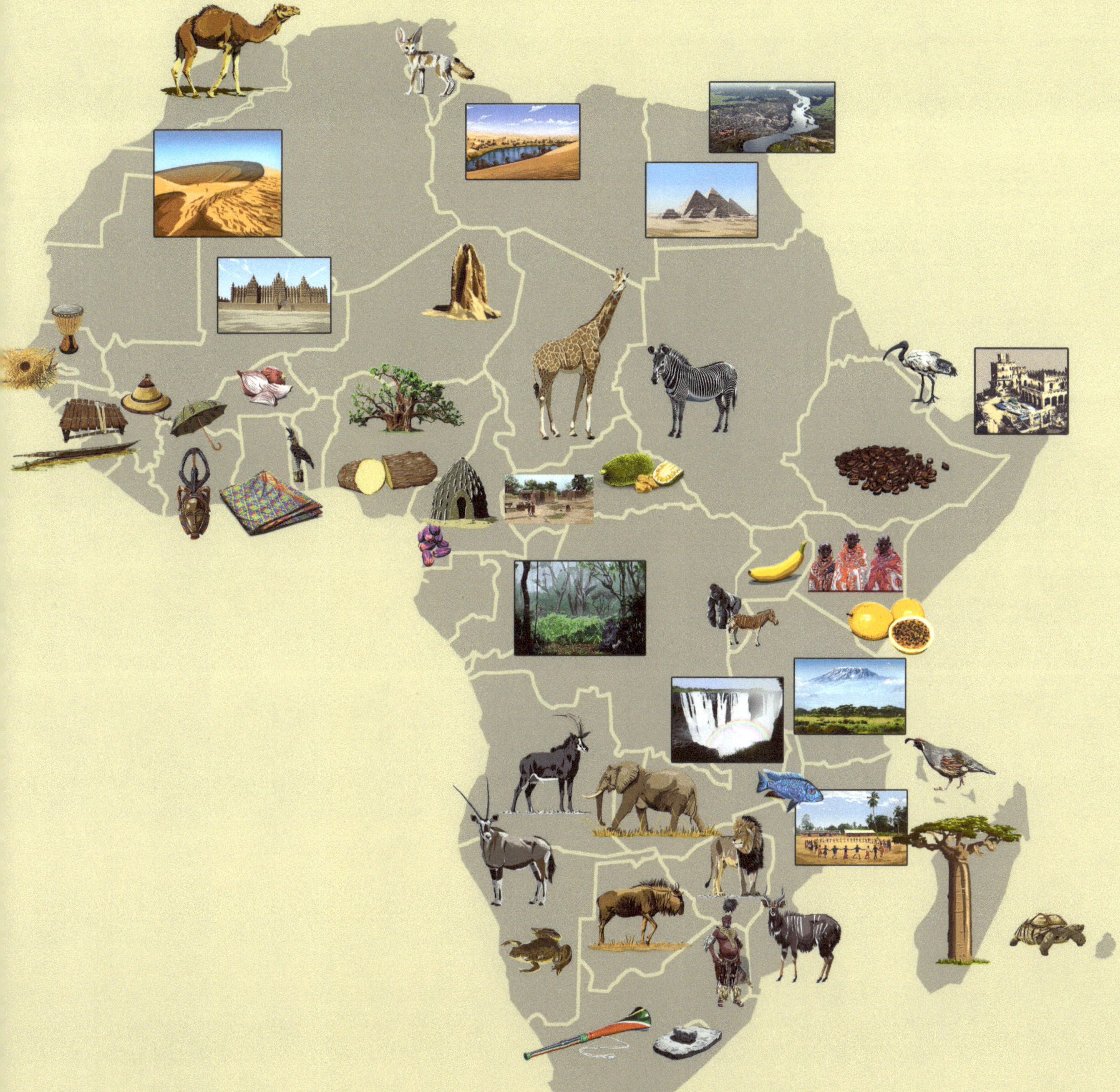

one

1

one

One Tree

2

two

Two Lions

3

three

Three Huts

4

four

Four Turtles

5

five

Five Dancers

6

six

Six Mangoes

7

seven

Seven Drums

8

eight

Eight Giraffes

9

nine

Nine Flowers

10

ten

Ten Elephants

1 2 3
4 5 6
7 8 9
10

Glossary

Baobab (bey-oh-bab): A great big tree that has the fattest tree trunk of them all found in tropical Africa, with hard fruits shaped like a ball.

Iroko (Iro-ko): A very strong reddish-brown wood tree found in Africa which can be used to make furniture for you and for me. And some even believe it has magic powers.

Kilimanjaro (kil-uh-muh-n-jahr-oh): A sleeping volcano which is Africa's highest point and quite a sight; you can even hike up it if you're not afraid of the height.

Kente (ken-tey): A fabric from the land of Ghana which is very colourful and is worn as a symbol of African pride.

Maasai (muh-sahy): In the east African highlands, these people can be found, they are a warrior tribe, and their traditional singing is a cultural sound.

Pyramid (pir-uh-mid): These great triangular structures are found up in Egypt; they are ancient and were used as tombs.

Stone (stohn): Pieces of rock were broken into pieces and used to grind grains and spices.

Safou (sah-foo): A fruit tree native to Africa, also called the bush pear or plum, with fruit that has a creamy, buttery flavour.

Timbuktu (tim-buhk-too): A town in Western Africa found in the Mali land by the Niger River and Sahara desert and is mostly covered with sand.

Ubuntu (uu-boon-tuu): This word means humanity and is a South African name; it means you should treat everyone with kindness and all the same.

Vuvuzela (voo-voo-zel-uh): A long plastic horn that makes a loud monotone sound; these are popular with fans and can be found on most sports grounds.

Zulu (zoo-loo): A member of the Nguni people who live in South Africa who used to live in clans. Zulu is also a language that is spoken by many in the African lands.

Did you know?

The longest river in the world is found in Africa; it is called the Nile River. It flows through ten countries.

Africa is the hottest continent on the Earth. The highest temperature ever recorded was over 130 °F or 54.44 °C

The world's largest and tallest land animals are found in Africa; they are the elephant and the giraffe.

The Victoria Falls in Zimbabwe are one of the Seven Wonders of the World.

The Sahara Desert is the world's largest hot desert. It crosses eleven nations.

The hippo is Africa's deadliest animal.

The largest island off Africa is called Madagascar. It is where most of the vanilla comes from.

There are over 1000 languages spoken in Africa.

More people speak French in Africa than they do in France.

Egypt is the most popular place for people to visit in Africa, and it also has Africa's largest city, which is called Cairo.

www.ingramcontent.com/pod-product-compliance
Lightning Source LLC
Chambersburg PA
CBHW060820270326
41930CB00003B/99

9 780990 875789